LETTERS

from a

STRANGER

p o e m s

LETTERS
from a
STRANGER
poems

JAMES TIPTON
with a foreword by
ISABEL ALLENDE

CONUN
DRUM
PRESS

AN IMPRINT OF BOWER HOUSE

DENVER

Letters from a Stranger: Poems. Copyright © 1998 and 2019 by James Tipton. All rights reserved. Printed in Canada. No part of this book may be used or reproduced in any manner whatsoever without written permission except in the case of brief quotations embodied in critical articles and reviews. Bower House books may be purchased with bulk discounts for educational, business, or sales promotional use. For in-formation, contact Bower House P.O. Box 7459 Denver, CO 80207 or visit BowerHouseBooks.com.

Designed by Margaret McCullough

Library of Congress Information Available Upon Request
ISBN 978-0-9657159-3-5

10 9 8 7 6 5 4 3 2

ACKNOWLEDGMENTS

I wish to thank the editors of the following magazines in which current or earlier versions of some of these poems first appeared: "In This Solitude Which Is Never Really Solitude" and "What Is This Place I Have Come To?," *South Dakota Review*; "Out of the Blue Breath of God," "I Want to Speak with the Blood that Lies Down," and "There Are Rivers of Oranges, Sweet," *American Literary Review;* "Watching Episodes of Unsolved Mysteries," *Pinyon Poetry;* "On This High Mesa I Keep a Low Profile" and "The God We Pray to When We Think We Pray," *Writers' Forum;* "These Awkward Efforts to Be Alive," *East West Journal;* "So Many Times I Have Felt the Sea Rising," *Messages from the Heart*; "So Many Times I Have Felt the Sea Rising," *The Sunday Suitor;* "This Story is About Fire and Destruction," *Columbia Poetry Review;* and "Do Not Look for Me Then, in the Tiny Dust," *High Plains Literary Review.*

Several poems were included in the anthology, *Bleeding Hearts* (Aurum, 1998), edited by Michelle Lovric: "After Years of Listening, A Stone Comes to Life," "I Want to Speak with the Blood that Lies Down," "I Wanted You in the Kitchen of My Heart," and "So Many Times I Have Felt the Sea Rising." "I Want to Speak with the Blood that Lies Down," "I Wanted You in the Kitchen of My Heart," and "There are Rivers of Oranges, Sweet" appeared in the anthology, *The Geography of Hope* (Conundrum Press, 1998), edited by David J. Rothman.

Two appeared in *Prize Poems* (Pennsylvania Poetry Society, 1998): "Who Are You, Goddess of the Green Night?" and "First, When She Was Talking, I Heard No Sound." Several appeared in a chapbook, *The Wizard of Is* (Bread & Butter Press, 1995): "Those Evenings When All of God's Conundrums," "The Poem Rises Up," (previously published as "The Poem Rises Up, Out of the Sand, Out"), "All God's Evenings Got Wings," "What Brilliant Dementia Drives Me," "Like Some Bituminous and Temporary Delight," "I Want to Speak with the Blood that Lies Down," "What Is This Place I Have Come To?," "There Are Rivers of Oranges, Sweet," "In This Solitude Which is Never Really Solitude," and "On This High Mesa I Keep a Low Profile."

I also wish to thank the many wonderful people who have been important to me and to these poems. Some of them are: Isabel Allende and Willie Gordon, Michelle Lovric, Jim Daniels, Bob and Gerri Jaeger, Chauk Lester, Mike and Claudia Delp, Jim Grabill and Marilyn Burki, Nick and Nancy Arky, Douglas and Mabel Anderson, Arcangelo Riffis, Roberto and Katia Forns-Broggi, Cherylyn Van Kirk, Fred Terry, Francisco Trujillo, Rhonda Claridge, Schuyler Greenleaf, Henry and Barbara Lugh, Woody Hildebrant, Richard and Virginia Bodner, Lorin and Donna Swinehart, John and Maria Hicks, Luis and Maggie Lopez, Russell Rock, Grace Cavalieri, Terry Pickens, Henrietta Hay, Jane Piirto, William Palmer, Rosemerry Wahtola Trommer, Art Goodtimes, Lili Marín, Maeve McGrath; and, of course, my loving and supportive family, my mother and father, Ruth and Robert Tipton, and my two sisters, Nancy Davis and Peggy Lutz.

A special thanks is due my perceptive and conscientious friend and editor, David J. Rothman, and to his patient and diligent assistant Catherine Sherrer.

For Isabel

CONTENTS

Contents

One day, during the summer of 1994, I received a letter from a stranger. He said he was writing to me from the top of the Andes, and described an infinite horizon of purple mountains, indigo skies, and the abysmal beauty of the ancient stones of Machu Picchu, where the spirits of dead Incas still roam. In that impressive setting, the stranger was reading one of my books, and maybe the story resonated with that landscape and he felt compelled to get in touch with me. A few weeks later I received another letter from him, this time from a little town in the mountains of Colorado. His letter contained an unusual gift: a story. Not long ago, he said, a woman was taken to an alcoholic rehabilitation hospital in western Colorado, so drunk that she could not remember her own name. She had been found on the railway tracks making love with a man that she had picked up in a bar. She was wearing a torn wedding dress and had a bouquet of dead flowers in her hands... "I will find out the rest of the story, if you are interested," offered the stranger.

I was hooked, not only by the fascinating mystery of that woman, but mainly by the man who had the intuition to send me that precious gift. How did he know that I could never resist such a bait? I replied to his letter immediately and that is how my friendship with Jim Tipton began.

It was a bad time in my life, a time of mourning and darkness. My daughter had died, I had written a painful memoir and I had the feeling that there was nothing else for me to do in this world. But Jim Tipton kept on writing to me, even when I failed to answer. His poems started to come, one by one, several a week, and I found myself waiting for the mail with a secret anxiety that I did not want ot admit even in the silence of my heart. Slowly, something happened to me. I began to open myself to that voice that was most certainly masculine and strong, but also tender and sensuous. Often the voice would almost be insane, and precisely in those moments it touched me the most. Jim Tipton's poems would go deep down inside my sorrow and swim like small fish. Sometimes they seemed to surface while I was driving to my office in

Sausalito, or walking in the forest where I scattered my daughter's ashes. The poems brought me to their soft light, and gave me back the love of words that I had almost forgotten. Some lines of the poems stayed with me for days; they were like shadows, like sounds I heard in sleep, like ships that slip unnoticed into the port at night. This poet seemed as solitary as I was at that time, but he had found the solace and peace that I did not have. He walked in nature as I did, but while I was crying, he was noticing the smells of honey and sage, the shapes of rocks and trees, the golden specks in the eyes of his dog, the murmur of bees, all those little things that suddenly were transformed into reassurances because the observer was a poet. Extraordinary poems! So simple and so honest, like an arrow straight to my longing.

And thus, one poem at a time, our friendship steadily evolved and the stranger became a dear friend. I have a very big basket where I keep our correspondence. When I bought it, I told the sales person that the basket was for love letters and she smiled mockingly. "You are an optimist," she said. "No, I am practical," I replied. It filled up fast. Soon I will have to go back for another one. In the meantime Jim Tipton kept on sending me handmade candles, books, stories and poems. I replied with parcels of exotic teas of exotic names and homemade cookies. He also sent me his picture: a tanned man with sharp blue eyes, white hair, and a beard, the captain of a pirate ship. At the end of 1995, for Christmas, he finally came to visit me in California. I recognized him immediately at the airport: he smelled of honey. We hugged each other with the easy confidence of a brother and a sister. All my family was reunited that Christmas, including my parents who had come from Chile. I introduced Jim Tipton as the man who writes like Pablo Neruda.

During almost a decade of life in the United States, I have rarely found any contemporary poems in English that have the wild and tumbling images that are found in the poetry of my country. Chile is the land of poetry. I was brought up reciting it by heart. Poetry is like bread and water for the Chilean people, *it does not belong to those who write it, but to those who need it,* as someone once said. And who doesn't need poetry? Like Neruda, Jim Tipton is a man of the heart and the senses. It is rare to find poetry that has that cascading energy and purity.

How can I write about these things? I have never been very interested in academic insights, and I find most literary scholarship quite boring. I much prefer to read stories and poems for the simple pleasure that they bring to my soul. Some days a window opens by itself, and poetry comes in, and something returns to our lives that we did not know that we lost. Then every fragrance becomes incense, and we see the world in a different light, and the milk that we put on our cereal takes on the flavor of some forgotten love potion. Every time I get a letter from that stranger that is now my friend, I hear his voice like rushes of wind from the deserts of western Colorado. If I close my eyes, I can see him walking with Ananda, his beloved dog, under the brilliant heavens and listening in the dark for another poem. And I am thankful that this man who is almost a hermit, stubbornly refusing to live any life but his own, has chosen me for a friend.

When Jim told me that he intended to publish this collection of poems, I asked him if I could write a brief foreword because I need to share my gratitude with his readers. Jim Tipton's poems have accompanied me like faithful nightingales in the long nights that followed my daughter's death. Now I am back on my feet. I have the will to live and the joy to write again. Now I can read Jim's poetry with new delight, lingering on the images, the magic and the language. I cherish these *Letters from a Stranger* that talk of ordinary experiences—wings, canyons, rocks, flesh—but mainly that other extraordinary experience... love. These poems are written by a man who was born to write poetry.

Isabel Allende

I

Mientras escribo estoy ausente
y cuando vuelvo ya he partido.

When I am writing I am not here
and when I return I have already left.

—Pablo Neruda, "Muchos Somos"

THOSE EVENINGS WHEN ALL OF GOD'S CONUNDRUMS

Those evenings when all of God's conundrums
arrive at once, I look for something solid,
like the cook, caught in the lick of thyme,
when she looks into her red soup, pondering
the interminable tomatoes of the past,
or like the old man in the cathedral in Cuzco,
muttering under his breath, "Jesus be damned,
and the one good eye of the Pope too!"

These evenings when God's conundrums arrive,
I remember the dead universities,
the knowledge that grew there like extra fingers,
until the hand was no longer able
to find a glove that fit against the cold;
I remember the words that fell like brilliant rain,
dazzling the dark out of the hair,
turning it this unruly and early white.

These evenings when all of God arrives at once—
conundrum and clumsy shepherd, three-personed and
inconclusive, like water filled to the brim with jugs—
He asks me whether I have any wool,
whether I have any weather left in me
to turn this drift of sail to land.
Only one answer comes to hand:
"Yes Sir, yes Sir, three bags full."

When all the evenings conundrum together
to this single lost star moment,
God gathers around me—and I stare,
with the intensity of the feeble minded,
at some gap in space that leaves the ganglia flattened,
a gap that like some heavy iron passes
over these buttery cells, until even the very soul
seems to be only breakfast for some imbecilic chorus.

"We'll be together yet, *mi campesina*," I sing,
while guns and conundrums bugle out God
to the winds not yet born, to the lazy hearts,
to the ladder of day, to the fetal angels,
to the distances that always repeat themselves,
to mouths that open like sockets of eyes,
to the delirious roses that bloom on the cheeks of love,
to the herds on high, the horse that swallowed the sea.

That campesina conundrum also is not satisfying,
arriving like a country Madonna, a fixture on a tomb,
like gold faucets in the homes of the wealthy,
that campesina, that piece of bread, that rosy God
always just out of reach, that benign and treacherous
presence that sighs out hope and the false peace
of future possibilities, that siren against which
I have hoarded the wax of bees.

These evenings when God's arrival
all at once conundrums, what I lack
in purity of spiritual intention I compensate for
with purity of desperation; and some compensation,
unexpected, sets in, like the subdued pain in the ring finger
from the bite of the Black Widow six weeks ago;
like the soft ecstasy that is sinking into me now
while I sip this delicate tea of mangos and marigolds
I received today in the mail from a stranger.

SOME DAYS I WAKE UP WALKING OVER THE DESERT

Some days I wake up walking over the desert
and see pieces of me everywhere:
in these knuckles of ancient trees,
in that tumbleweed of soul in this spring wind,
in the tiny flowers rooted on heart rock.
Even a piece of sleep that I thought was mine
flew in the blue wing of day out of a dead limb.

Ah, this gathering and gathering of self,
this brown joy in the eyes of a beloved dog,
this dust that dances into blossom,
this little notebook that is the earth,
this endless love that when we least expect it
knocks on our door and says
let the day begin.

Insisting with the only life I know
on some peace at the end of solitude
and desperation, I have arrived
here, at this desert place,
where a magic that few would want
rings light around me, where grace
comes toward me, one step at a time.

Out of the Blue Breath of God

Out of the blue breath of God the sea was made
and then the wild horses of the sea
and then the severed tongues and the rosaries
and the frightened hair on the arms of the dead.

I would like to rub oil with the odor of coconut
over the body of a woman I love;
I would like not to remember the news;
not remember limbs lying in the jungle,
the huge eyes of starving children.

I would like to leap out of this ack of rain and loneliness,
out of these damp clothes filled with stones,
out of this clumsy shrine, out of this room
where the phone rang every night for months
and no one was there.

I do not even know what occupation I have,
except for raising fourteen window shades each morning,
and lowering fourteen window shades each evening,
and blessing fourteen people who come to mind each morning
when I raise the shades and each evening when I lower them:
enemies, fools, lovers, strangers, pictures.

Sometimes I feel like I live in some eternal wake
for everyone who has died, or who has not lived,
or who lives, wrapped in some heavy web of lead,
and sometimes I wonder what somber soul is in me
singing its silent blessings to those who live,
as if by blessing I might raise them from the dead.

Do you remember that night when I sent you
the opera glasses, rescued for another kind of seeing?
And the full moon that night
that was shining through the stars of honey
lined along the windows?

And do you remember the islands submerged for centuries,
and the flowers that opened up like schools, and the fish
in the red sea of the western sun, and the thousand
years of hairshirts, and the bread that rose up like
water in the old well when we needed it most?

And the blessings carried by tiny bees,
and the lost angel in the forest I searched for in Ohio
when I was seven years old?
And the light that throbbed against me in the abandoned orchard?
And the two poems Neruda sent me that I gave away?

Do you remember all the letters I did not write to you,
and the house that was like a convent that had escaped,
and the spirits that lifted me out of the icy lake I had waded into
in Michigan one late February, up to my neck?

And do you remember the soul in the omphalos,
sliding out at birth, seeing its first clock,
and the ewe weeping for her lost lamb,
and the first cell of your body?

And do you remember that first sleep of the child born,
the eyes opening to a hazy room,
the fascinating sound of human voices,
the first fly you saw, and the taste of mushed fruit?
And do you remember the sweet smell of women,
and the first bird at the window,
and the delicate water over the eyes of strangers?

Is It True That I Lack Focus

Is it true that I lack focus, but I live each day
with the insane sweetness of honey,
and I live each night with stars
moving over the bed; it is true
that I have little money, but I know
the fragrance of sage after a rain
and the wild heart of the desert wind.

Several lives ago I was born in Ohio,
where I slept with the window always open,
with the moon curled in these arms
like a sacred breast; and always
in all the houses that surrounded me,
I listened to some tiny thing
that, like a fish in winter, survived.

Here, in the canyons of western Colorado,
many things once important to me
have departed, but I no longer stand
dying of thirst on lonely balconies;
I no longer suffer through bullies
whose blood drowns hope and love.
I find goodness now in every shape of day.

It is true that I remain clumsy, but
I have become a master at following whims—
and that has brought me to those I love,
our lives joined by this moon we dance around,
our hands stretching into the dark
like long loaves of bread,
sharing the wheat of the human heart.

THE POEM RISES UP

The poem rises up, out of the sand,
out of the desert grasses,
out of the hair of everything that sways,
that sings, even out of those lost
in the infirmaries of brains,
even out of the lost hand at the end of the arm
when one is deeply thinking,
even out of the lonely metaphysicians
who believe that what is sent out comes back to you,
who are confounded for those moments when they stare
at the hard eyes of Christ in the crucifixes
in the cathedrals in Lima and Cuzco.

What used to be God has become poem,
what used to be light has become the sand
that begins to surge under the feet
when one is walking at night, alone;
what used to be God has become bees,
has become the blood pools in the eyes
at sunset, has become the silence we always feel
when we look deeply into the tiny hearts
of the cells in the tiny hands
of the tiny girl named Maria,
selling scarves in the plaza, hugging the wool
like tiny dolls in winter.

What used to be God has become the wild stillness
which rises up like a wave without its ocean,
has become the wild language of those
who long to speak, like the tongues of lizards
rooted on the sunny rocks, has become the wild intensity
with which we watch bullets moving toward us,
until the bullets themselves are hardly moving—
and were we able to lift our heavy hands
we might hold them in their flight, might turn their sinister lead
into bread or into nuggets of living gold, might send them back,
until the very dust on the feet of the damned
might turn into the dew of oceans and diamonds.

What used to be love has become the sound we make
before we make sound, the seeing we do before
we become seeing, the matter that makes the fragrance
of lilacs or rose, the divinity that rises
out of this endless sage after a rain, the shapes a pen
makes on paper, the heart inside the letter
that becomes word, that becomes the ancient rocks
singing, undulating, themselves becoming breasts
washed in the milk of this full moon, this night
when the Wizard of Is is the only light,
and the only prayer this body, barely breathing
this mouth under this sky of love.

I WANT TO SPEAK WITH THE BLOOD THAT LIES DOWN

Yo quiero hablar con muchas cosas
y no me iré de este planeta
sin saber qué vine a buscar...

I want to speak with many things
and I will not leave this planet
without knowing what I came here to find...

—Pablo Neruda, "Bestiario"

I want to speak with the blood that lies down
each night to sleep inside your heart; I want to speak
with these words that procreate like rabbits
when I think of you; I want to speak with your virginal ribs,
with the hand inside; I want to devour the mud that mocks
all diamond flesh; I want to find a prayer that sticks,
a clock that ticks only love, a time
that turns this desperation into peace, a book
with the moon on every page that only we
can read together; I want to speak in one
interminable sentence that can be understood
in a single sitting; I want to speak with
the tired angels that live inside the shoulders
of tiny children; I want to speak with cripples
that meet in laundromats late at night looking
for little boxes of soap; I want to speak with
these clothes before I join them; I want to find
the delicate violet that rises out of the dead volcano;
I want to find the verb that shakes me loose,
the noun that is the place I live, the
comma that joins me with you; I want
to speak softly and thoroughly, and be clearly
in you; I want to speak with apples and honey
and silver and snow—I want everything to stop
for a moment destined for you and for me,

for a time when we, butchered at birth,
come back to life, rescued at last
like children in a miraculous fairy tale—
I want to speak with the dead, who move
like leaves in this night that blows its rapture
toward the dislocated sea; I want to speak
with the forgotten spring, with the light
in the dead comet; I want to speak with salt
and with the teeth I found in the desert and with
wounded silence, ravenous solitude;
I want to speak with Pablo Neruda and Christ,
and with the idiot brother of God, and with the tunnel
at the foot of the bed, with the corridors
of all longing; I want to speak with these long nights
of useless letters, with these boots that walk without me
when I rest, and with the spirits that shake these feet
when I lay me down to weep; I want to speak with the
thirsty rain, the lonely garbage, the tire that remembers
when it was a tree in Brazil; I want to speak with
the fragrance of sage that rises up, late into the night,
after a soft rain; I want to speak with cinnamon
and chocolate, and with windows that do not open,
and with the bag of hair in the shop of the old barber;
I want to speak with the dance that rises
in this body when, like a distant bell
come home, your letter rings in me whatever
matters; I want to whisper "love … love … love"
while this very hand is stretched to Sausalito,
cradling your heart in sleep.

AFTER YEARS OF LISTENING

After years of listening, a stone comes to life,
and the candle in the tiny grass;
and the night, like a wife, comes home;
a feather, in this touch of wind, flies back
to the lost bird, and everything I do not know
begins to sway at once.

I love these nights of irresistible somnambulance!
These nights when the wind blows its lullaby
to each lonely wing; I love this old body I walk in,
I love this dependable sage, this desert scent
I sink into when I rest; and suddenly I know
I will no longer apologize for loving you.

I whispered your name and the wind whinnied back.
All the horses of heaven are in the pasture tonight.

So Many Times I Have Felt the Sea Rising

So many times I have felt the sea rising
in my heart, when in my hands
I hold your letters, like singing nets of words
lifted out of some blue solitude for me alone.

So many times again I open your golden letters,
reading them to bees, to canyon walls,
to tiny lizards that dart like thoughts
through these deserts of perpetual loneliness.

So far away, so far, I felt, wanting to live at last
with only spirits, but oh, *dueña del amor,*
the feather I found, fallen from the angel's wing,
means nothing to me now.

BEING STUBBORN

Being stubborn is the only thing that ever
brought me love: being stubborn
and being alone, listening all the way down,
until the house in the wild desert wind
began to rise and what I thought was me
dropped, like a knot falling out of a tree.

We can walk a long time to find the moon again,
to find letters that read like answered prayers,
to find a face or two that turn a thought
to sacred water, to find the narrow place
where life says climb, climb until the song
inside the star is more than ancient memory.

In this rising of everything, all of our training
for the trails of ordinary fails us...fails us...
so that we may succeed in something higher
than confused dust and desperate lust;
and all our lives when listened to
have led us to this simple path.

I Want to Love You With Every Piece of This Body

I want to love you with every piece of this body:
I want these strong and simple hands to divine
each delicate sound inside of you; I want
these faithful legs to gallop at midnight
through the sleeping orchards of your heart;
I want these eyes, these singing eyes
that have survived the brutal clocks, the days
lost in daily space, to blossom in some high bed
of human heaven; I want these feet that never sleep
to wander in the deepest part of you, like ghosts
unchained, ecstatic in this desert sea;
I want this blood, this red tenderness,
to be your blanket; I want this brown and peasant face
to race through solitude and rock, until
with you at last *The Book of Moon* is read;
I want this tongue, that like some acrobat insane
tumbles toward you with what little words I have,
to sip some virgin secret that you hold;
I want this heart, in time both infinite and now,
to know the reason for the light in you that lifts me.

WHAT IF THE POEM WERE A SHOUT

What if the poem were a shout
out of the center of a dream?
What if the dream were a hand
that was inside a hand that was still
inside another hand and then you
were holding out your hand?
And what if when I began to kiss you
the moon you sat on was rocking
like a grandmother come home?

What if the dream were shouting
and the poem were a thicket
and then a cathedral or a tree
with a door that opens when I feel sad
and the dazzling light inside with no source,
and the steps that go down to the canyon,
and I decided then to go to Peru,
to the nude stone at Macchu Picchu
where the sluggish alphabet was born?

In July I climbed those ancient stones,
beyond the terraces, and sat watching
the sun rise through trapezoidal windows,
near what the Indians call
the hitching post of the sun.
When a golden butterfly landed
on the jeweled and silver cross
I was wearing, I remembered
that particular dream.

And what if the shouting were dreaming,
and the bullets moved toward me through
water, and I began weeping in sleep,
until two women began moving me back and forth,
feeding me with tenderness,
and I woke up alone and in love
with no particular person,
and hungry for hot chocolate
and buttered toast?

And what if with you—when I must
say clear things or sound insane—
the dream and the poem and the brain
race together in this strange water
that is the other side of sleep,
race like obscure conundrums
to no answer, this place where
for you and me and for God's sake
I pray hard the soul to wake.

WHAT IS THE STATE OF POETRY?

What is the state of Poetry?
Is it New York City where the words
are lonely tenants in green cement?
Is it the Amazon where there is a bird
with claws at the end of its wings, where
the Spanish explorer returned home with tales
of fierce women warriors?
Is it the hand that reaches
into the dark and pulls out bones of wishes?
Is it Cuzco where the earth quakes
and tumbles the Spanish structures built
on Incan walls where centuries later
you cannot fit a knife between the stones?

Is it the universities, where the lure of being
the latest talent turns hands once tender
into hard hammers of knowledge, where the wild shadows
long ago packed up their bags and hit the road?
What is the state of Poetry? Is it
a state of no-mind, where words drop
like rat shit into the kitchen drawers
of self-declared shamans, where commas
procreate like a large family of curved fingers,
hooking us toward them, where identities
strip themselves naked for our illumination
revealing only new identities, clothed in
intractable and decaying armor?

The State of Poetry. What is the country
of our longing, the thousand years of lips
broken loose looking for kisses in the desert,
looking for the God who does not go home
at the end of the party, at the end
of the clumsy throbbing of this confused blood?
What is this Colorado of language,
Ohio of family, Peru of sleep; what are
these roving bands of little towns,
these packs of cities wild for their own flesh,
these battered shirts of drying nouns,
these food lines of stumbling verbs; what are
these participles of atoms, these quantum hearts?

ANY POEM

Any poem
worth its salt
must have
the sea in it
and at least
a pinch
of sweet flesh,
and it probably
needs a couple
of stray dogs
and some green
jazz, and
those huge rocks
behind the house
we thought
were ordinary
until they surfaced
in our sleep,
and a poem needs
love, but simple,
like coarse mustard
on muenster cheese,
and some light,
like the first cell
that began
our bodies,
and some darkness,
like the center
of bread
before it begins
to rise,
and two strong legs
willing to run off
without us.

THERE ARE RIVERS OF ORANGES

There are rivers of oranges, sweet
like the autumn sun, sweet
like sand on the doubloon
found at the bottom of sleep,
like the sweet stars we delicately peel,
like the roots of acorn squash,
like the eyes of the jaguars in Peru.

When we deeply imagine
we no longer imagine at all,
but dive, at last, naked and alive,
into the flesh of oranges, into
the steaming jungle, into words
that hang like orange rain,
like love just before it happens.

It is everything we ever wanted
to remember, like empty orange
file folders labeled "Careers," like
the lover who walks backwards
through every shift of love until
he arrives home, to the place
where what is seen inside is what is.

There the orange mind bursts
like a village of chrysanthemums
gone mad, or gathered together
for mass, praising
the orange hands of God, praising
the saffron eyes of the flower saints,
praising the hearts in the tiny seeds.

II

… quise nadar en las más anchas vidas,
en las más sueltas desembocaduras …

*… I want to swim in the deepest lives,
in the waters most swift …*

—Pablo Neruda, "Alturas de Macchu Picchu"

II

In the Higher Saloons of Canyons and Oats

for James Grabill

In the higher saloons of canyons and oats
I read your bread, the brown beach where the blue word
rushes in, recedes, where ants,
too close for safety, rush to build
their tiny pyramids, where the ocean inside of the hand
shakes its Dolphin locks, lies down to sing inside our flesh,
remembering old country songs out of the desert
at the bottom of the sea, remembering
the humming monsters, remembering
the rain that cackles in late Autumn, and the dust
inside the drop of water.

In the Grabill grass, under the rib of the moon,
light continues to rush forth,
like the flowers on the arm of the foreman,
like tattoos on windows in winter,
like the yellowed news in the eyes of ancient women,
like the swirl of sun in the bodies of bees,
like tree food stored in the body of the house,
like the saxophone the drunken angel was playing
on the fire escape in San Francisco,
like the wings of the spider when it begins its web,
like the metaphor no longer hallucinatory.

And in the James light, the grave of everything that lives
lifts up the crates, lifts up the empty bowls that fill
before our very touch, a world that lives
because we feed it bone and corn,
because we love it into blossom,
because we know the crow heart, to coyote heart,
the heart of the old camp, the heart of the worn doll
I saw in the museum, named "Arapahoe, circa 1880,"
because we know our lost destiny
will be returned at last, born to us by a stranger
in a taxi painted the color of red-tailed hawks.

And in the Hotel Manger, the child is born;
and the wise men on trains that have been running
through centuries of Decembers
stop in every little whistle town and pass
tickets through the houses, run their long arms
through sleeping bodies, caressing the light
in form, until the cells that usually thicken in the night
begin to quicken, like milk in the body of the child
before words, like the candle in the voice before
we believe it is sound, like the ore in the stars
that became our bodies.

The Brain Washes Ashore, a Curdled Nautilus

The brain washes ashore, a curdled nautilus,
and the day begins. These thick words,
the only wife I have, wake up inside this body
and take me to public places, where a dislocated
geography grinds people in its deadly map,
a map that has no stars, only Monday morning,
set in motion by the shop or office clock,
the factory by the broken sea.

What poem, in these cities where money weeps,
is worth even a dollar? What poem, in this time
of sleeping hearts hunched toward their tiny visions,
is willing to impale itself upon the delirious day;
what poem is willing to run naked through the streets,
to die of cold, of impossible loneliness?
What poem is willing to send its long tongue
toward the sad heart on the lone coast?

Paris, boy that he was, was willing to trade
power, wealth, nobility, honor, for one sweet thing:
the woman that he loved. But where now is passion?
Passion for anything that might lift the heart
out of shadow, out of hushed bones, out
of the desolate waters that wash over our century,
out of the unreliable regularity of the day-to-day,
out of the tombs we die in that we call home.

And so, this morning, I think of the petrified hands,
and of tenderness, and of clothes
walking around looking for themselves,
and of the strange exhaustion that rises out of this century,
and of the endless food that never fills us,
and of the moon we have never seen,
and of the lonely poems that still kneel down,
late at night, in the old cathedral of the heart.

A Shuddering Geography Pulls the Dead Sentences

A shuddering geography pulls the dead sentences
through the body, and the spirit, that is destined
to be pure, says she is not here.

Slightly humiliated by the roses
that still want to gather under the eyes, I extend kisses,
at midnight, to the salt of her distant body.

I devour tea in sleep, and manuals of bright,
to tip the surface back to peace,
the ordinary, to light and quick devotions.

At a late hour, the sheep were calling to each other,
and I walked their narrow paths through clover
also calling, over and over, for finer weather.

First, When She Was Talking, I Heard No Sound

First, when she was talking, I heard no sound,
then, like water falling far down the canyon,
I heard her say her name, but it was more
than human name, more than alphabet at birth.

It was like a fragrance around a camp at night,
like a sign we make when no one is looking,
like a hand inside a hand that sometimes
stretches out of sleep, or waves at strangers.

That evening when I climbed the long moon
to home, I held that name, like I hold
a sound inside the body, like I hold
the mountains lightly on this back.

A Stray God, or a Thump in the Night

A stray God, or a thump in the night,
or a cathedral bell far off
begins its steady prayer,
coming closer and closer until
I wake on this damp hill and realize
the bell that woke me
is this very heart,
a prodigal sound come home.

Putting consciousness together, I do
simple things: "two and five make four,
and then ten"; still nothing, nothing but
the mother of breathing
beneath me, nothing but the fragrance
of hill, the heat of stars in the cool night,
nothing but the rivers inside pulled awake
by the Pope on the moon, by the mist
at the edge of a woman in another galaxy.

I Watched at Low Tide Your Breasts Rise

I watched at low tide your breasts rise.
I watched every effort that you made
to be beautiful for me. Even though
I was a stranger, your body moved
for me alone, like the hope
that moved behind the mirror
that did not find you beautiful at all.

What a strange thing, that longing
to be beautiful, the sweet pretense
and secret weeping, the doubt inside
that rose against the right you had
to boldly wear that pink bikini
and walk alone on what you thought
was sand deserted.

At what age did you know—
for certain—that you
never would be beautiful,
never shine yourself
into the poems of lovers,
never have the sultry bliss
that beauty by itself can bring?

I took you home in thought
that moment by the sea,
and lived a life with you,
your homely face casting its desire
each winter night by candle,
your body arched
in clumsy grace and love.

But I did not tell you this,
I did not speak at all,
pondering your sweet attempts
to bend and search for shells,
to move with all the sensual delight
your awkward dreams
could teach you.

Now, months later, this autumn night
in Colorado, I write this awkward
poem for you—some clumsy art
I struggle with—because
that longing in you
was so beautiful and pure
you touched this tired heart.

WHEN I STAND VERY STILL

When I stand very still, a dance begins
inside this body, and a thousand fishes,
disguised as words, leap up in the blood,
toward who knows what celestial mating waters.

When I stand very still, the mother of moons
and turquoise and bare feet begins to sing;
old chairs leave for good, and the tiny cells
swell up like grapes just before they become wine.

When I stand very still, the air, upon close inspection,
reveals sounds as ancient as salt, as ancient
as those soft stars that brush against the heart
when we are in love.

When I stand very still, all reason washes away,
the dead springs come back to life,
a thousand guitars play in the distance;
and, in this early summer, you are with me.

I Wanted You in the Kitchen of My Heart

I wanted you in the kitchen of my heart;
and there, after many cold lunches,
I found you; and there, like herbs
undressing in soup, I came to love you;
and there, like a delicate tea
of mangoes and marigolds your mouth
opened, and your words, flecked with gold
and the eroticism of your Latin blood,
flowed, like the blood I longed for, into me.

And how could I lose you among these cups
and spoons, among these golden candles,
these jars of honey lined along the window?
And what forget-me-nots in winter
tie me to you still? I could die in this bread
I have made without you. For you I would burn
this dry brain for incense; I would
serve you the wine inside the night; I would
drink the sea to give you salt.

A Blizzard is Flying Around the House

A blizzard is flying around the house; the Neruda book
I want to read lies in pieces banded together
in the blue truck in the bee garage;
the old tongue of God is rubbery tonight.

I have not eaten yet today: I want to open
a soup can labeled "Angels with Rice,"
or "God Chowder," "Beans of Heaven,"
"Heart Stew," "Cream of the Goddess."

It happens that I have been hungry for a long time;
it happens that often I would exchange this celestial solitude
for the deep sleep of the day I was born,
for the tiny bed hidden next to her heart.

It happens that often I would trade
every word I ever knew for one sip
of divine dew, for one eternal kiss,
for one moment of irrefutable bliss.

It happens that often, around others, I lie down
among their disordered sounds, their
submerged dining rooms, enduring
the din of day, the spikes against the back.

No monk, I live monastic, furiously wandering,
shivering in sleep, surrounded by corpses
of angels, by perforated saints, by grief,
by language, by garlands discarded by God.

It happens that a string still ties me to the end
of the wing of the long kite
held in the hand of the lonely boy
who wanted to be a bird.

Her Body Stuck Out Like a Thumb

Her body stuck out like a thumb,
lonely for a ride, and I,
easy prey for a stray thing,
stopped to let her in.

She was a breed, she told me,
casually, as if it were a region
in Colorado where she lost
her pet crow named Jesus.

She had been waiting, she said,
for me, or someone exactly like me,
for a long time, a life, standing
at abandoned stations, praying.

The desert roads I drive at night
often turn to nothing, but I love them,
like I love the interminable dust of stars
and scent of sage that is the true direction.

But in her eyes I saw the Amazon bird
that has claws at the ends of its wings,
and the corpses of little children
stuffed with cocaine to smuggle across borders.

Her desert was another desert;
the spirits in this desert were not
her spirits, and so I had to both hurt
and bless this destined union, and let her go.

I have wanted a woman for a long time.
I know that in this strange galaxy of flesh,
like the long hair of pollen, wearing
a skirt of Navajo red, she waits for me.

In Towns Made of Steel

In towns made of steel the air
begin to rust; at night the young girls
bathe and bathe, bewitched
by the possibilities of distant
towns made of grass.

In coastal towns where the sea birds,
wearing their capes of oil,
walk like old men dragging a heavy past,
boys play in the evening, praying secretly
for taxis the color of dolphins.

In one western city, the peregrine falcons
that were imported to eat the pigeons,
have vanished; and the telephone wires,
harmoniums out of India, hum
themselves out of town.

In the little town that is a diner
on the Utah desert, truck drivers
passing through listen patiently
to the homely waitress
talk about her amethyst crystals.

In sophisticated cities, the sexual militants
line up like lemmings,
their eyes rolling like confused oysters,
their feet walking ahead of them,
like scouts, looking for the promised land.

In all these places, the confused night remains bright
with confounding light, the day remains dim,
harder to remember than a chalk board
one particular day in first grade,
harder to remember than the first taste of water.

And we, in this town we make when we think
of each other, listen to these hearts beating
like bells under water,
and worship the flowers in words
like bees lost in old Calcutta.

Like Some Bituminous and Temporary Delight

Like some bituminous and temporary delight
her dark eyes led me to her jangled
light, her gibberish of metaphysical juice,
her lubricitous new age brain, bright
with the smoke of creative reason.

But in those eyes inside her eyes,
the sea was ringing, and the green
wave of the dragon flew in summer,
and the horned frog, the oyster bed,
the crippled crow who learned to talk.

In those eyes inside was something black
and pure, like a tiny obsidian keepsake
lost in the mountains, like the whole round heaven
those nights when the stars are tired,
like the soft dark at the center of sleep.

Inside those eyes inside, like a garden
at night, something sprouted which was not
light, some wild and ruminant power,
some opal of the incipient soul,
proud, ancient, and sufficient.

What Brilliant Dementia Drives Me

for Douglas Anderson

What brilliant dementia drives me
to these manic poems, to these
configurations of night,
these concatenations of lost light,
these tiny wings, these words
that tumble like lonely sailors
in San Francisco into some
sweet harbor hardly remembered
in the dim of day?

Decades now of *Uncollected Poems*
pile in this dark memory, papers
I pack without thinking whenever I move,
like women I have almost forgotten,
like sly mermaids just out of reach
in a slippery sleep, like ancient villages
where it is rumored words walk
with their hands open, like the moon
riding high on a razorback hog
through the hazy autumns of heaven.

One Night I Picked Up in a Bar

One night I picked up in a bar
a woman named Poetry,
and she was drunk, or I was drunk,
or the world itself was drunk;
but at any rate I took her home
and listened to her.

Now, you may be thinking, she had
golden breasts and golden thighs,
and in a sense you are correct.
Perhaps she was some
long forgotten lonely goddess
who through what strange shift in time
had surfaced in a pool hall,
surprised to be alive, to be admired.

I, to the end, lover of all forgotten things,
had seen her there, had loved her,
and in the clumsy way
I sometimes have with women
seduced her heart.

Ah... the muscled men who wanted her,
who watched amazed, were nothing then,
while I, the local fool, finessed my way
into her panties, finding
in that lap of language some ancient thing
so damp and lovely that the gods
of Greece and Rome tore out their hair.

These Awkward Efforts to Be Alive

These awkward efforts to be alive,
to wade, through our own debris,
toward shore, toward other people,
we take too seriously.

Our ships wreck, and we survive;
our hearts, stolen by pirates,
are not ransomed; but we
cannot weep forever for these lost things.

The sea, not the ship, is our mother.
The waves are never clumsy.
They know when to break,
to give up, to go back.

III

…yo tengo que ir mucho más lejos
y tengo que ir mucho más cerca…

*…I have to go much farther
and I have to go much closer…*

—Pablo Neruda, "Bestiario"

III

What Is This Place I Have Come To?

What is this place I have come to?
This river with no water, still flowing,
this back road to wisdom, this old mesa
where I feel driven to write to everyone
who lives, where this latest hallucination
of the heart starts again to hope?

What is this place I have come to?
This land of crows and golden eagles,
coyotes and the night wind weeping,
this place where every word ever spoken
in the universe speaks now,
where these golden skies walk to heaven?

What is this place I have come to?
This life with little focus, these nights
when wit flies into a storm
without a co-pilot, and words quicken
in the thick mind, and at the slightest touch
gold falls out of the Rabbit Brush?

What is this place I have come to, where
caught in God's own curfew I wander
through this late house, realizing
longing is the hardest thing to give up:
these years of longing to protect
the diamond wing of the gossamer child?

WHO ARE YOU, GODDESS OF THE GREEN NIGHT

Who are you, Goddess of the Green Night,
of the sultry ocean of sleep,
the hair of the dawn air?
Who are you, so casually possessing the bodies
of a thousand beautiful women,
young girls waiting for buses,
proud and unconscious women,
brutal women of diamond flesh, women
with golden fish in their legs, women
with lost voices, who are you?

Who are you, who have brought me so much misery,
so much joy? Who are you, huntress and hunted,
mistress and pure water, who are you—
my only real occupation, my sordid cross,
my poison and my song,
my solitary journey, my jeweled gypsy,
my eternal actress, my persistent ruin,
my voluptuous saint, my very soul traveling
through stained glass, my strange destiny invoked
the moment before each breath?

Who are you, with your passionate indifference,
your obscure language, your touch
like a thought turned phosphorescent,
your mouth almost visible, your eyes
like distant headlights in a heavy fog,
your nipples sprouting out of the rosy soil
known only to those who do not sleep,
your milk rushing into me when I see you
walking in a body, you who stood silently
beside me, the day I was born.

The Day I Was Born Was the Day

for Schuyler Greenleaf

The day I was born was the day
I began to fall in love with everything,
and particularly with the light,
with how it waved to me at dusk,
with how it rose after a summer rain
into the heart of that little boy,
with how it curled deep
in the centers of the flowers,
how it lived in little jars of honey.

I remember the day in the abandoned orchard
when the Angel of Light stood beside me;
and I remember the wild and lovely light
that wrapped itself around certain women,
so bright I could no longer see them;
I remember the light that lurked in language,
and I remember how much I loved words,
wanting to know them well before I spoke,
although I did not speak until I was three years old.

I remember how painful it has always been
to appear to be like others, how hard
I have had to work to dance in that world;
and I remember how much I loved
to be alone, and I remember
new leaves in late spring,
and corn smiling, and bees,
and the little creek I carried home
and tucked in bed beside me.

Even now, I find a few certain strangers
who come to me with light lingering
around them before they speak;
and when I leave them I remember that light,
and sometimes a piece of conversation,
with you, for example, about Costa Rica, and Peru,
and Spanish learned outside of schools.
I had to stop talking with you then,
or I would have given you everything I have.

WHAT IF, WHEN WE HELD EACH OTHER

What if, when we held each other, our flesh
became consciousness itself?
What if our flesh commingled
became the mother of light
and sound, the vast word,
the ocean forgotten at birth?

What if, when we held each other,
the skin between us slipped away,
and our old exasperated tongues
turned into everything that heals,
into one long kiss, the kiss that started
when the universe began.

What if, when we held each other,
nothing survived but one shared breath,
nothing survived but the sweet odors
of gentle and tempestuous love,
nothing survived but our sensual hearts
singing the only song there is.

Do Not Look for Me Then, in the Tiny Dust

Do not look for me then, in the tiny dust
that survives each ancient breath,
do not look for me in the mermaids
who float in the dark air, like seeds,
longing for heavy rains, and do not
look for me in this skeleton
that has left the reservation, or in the
ore that cascades out of your hair
when you are weary; and do not
look for me in the names that shape
our lives, the words that rustle like
clothes in abandoned closets, and do
not look for me in these hands that
wander deliriously over the rosary
of your body, and do not
look for me in these eyes
suspended on the branches
of brain, do not look for me
in this kiss that gallops along the shore
of your thoughts, or in
the humming of the bees
content in hexagrams, or in the husks
of other times, or in the wisdom
that bears down upon us
like a Mack truck, or in the radio station
contained in each atom, or in the
cemetery of all desires, or in the
saffron odor of saints, or in the
sweet juice at the center
of the kernel of brown rice, and
do not look for me in the meaning
we have wrapped around things,
or in the bag of hair the old barber
drags to the back room,
or in the uncluttered sleep of infants,

or in the x-ray vision of dolphins,
or in the cards that cast about,
seeking their own fortune, or in
the uniform of sex, or in the margins
of manuscripts in progress, the
poems that rattle in the carved gourd,
and do not look for me
in the boy with grey hair who
remembers the mica
that flaked like the pages
of angels when the earth
was being formed this very moment.

People Always Think I Suffer

People always think I suffer some spiritual discipline
when I tell them I wake each day at dawn.
Little do they know I have a cat, named Gosi,
who dances off the bed and tells me,
in a language surpassing clocks,
it is time to go outside and hunt the day.

People always think I suffer some spiritual discipline
when I tell them I work on poetry every day;
but how can I tell them the secret:
there is no discipline ... to me it is
like eating donuts or butter cookies,
like being in bed with exotic women.

People always think I suffer some spiritual discipline
when I go walking every day, hand in hand
with a book of Chinese love poems,
or a collection of Buddhist proverbs,
and with a golden dog named Ananda,
and with the child who still lives inside of me.

And so, although suffering is very fashionable,
I make no pretence now toward suffering,
nor toward discipline, preferring
the wild silence of these sacred canyons,
the solitude of the deep word,
this universe of infinite bread.

When I First Came Into This Desert Space

When I first came into this desert space
this heart was tired, these feet
had forgotten how to be feet,
deep in this body were bullets, festering;
and the desire to love someone
for a thousand years was almost dead.

A healing sometimes happens
when we least expect it, in the honey
that falls out of the sun into flowers,
in the measureless bed where one remembers
those he loves, in the tiny shovels
that sift through the dark for secret things.

Too old to become a hero, I walk
through sage and watch the stars
dissolve the corners of the night;
I put one ear against a hive of bees
to hear the sound of *om*, the old poem
the universe is always singing.

Tonight, Love, let us rub our aging souls
against each other to make fire,
let us listen to the words that wander
through our bodies, let us serenade
the longings of our souls
with sacred sounds and silence.

Sometimes the Fragrance of Honey and Beeswax

Sometimes the fragrance of honey and beeswax
follows me into sleep, and I know then, for certain,
on those nights legs will blossom, breasts
will touch their rosy faces to mine,
and all the women I love will come to me.
It is like spring when we least expect it,
like the rivers that rush through the canyons
after a long drought, like the intoxicating memories
that suddenly light candles deep inside the body.

I know for certain, then, that there is something
in night that is not night, that is not sleep
and that is not waking, something that is singing,
that is bringing gifts to me, something so intense
that even time itself is not secure
in the presence of this flowering of navels,
this room with bowls of peaches soaking in cognac,
with wedding dresses piled in the corner,
this bed with the inexhaustible perfume of those I love.

I know then, for certain, that I will remain
faithful to the sensual soul of every woman
who in this undulating dark slumbers toward me
oblivious to directions she learned at school,
no longer seeking anything but the sweet wind
blowing through her heart, no longer seeking
anything but the bread that rises up
in her delicious body, and honey
dripping like sweet dew.

MEANING STILL ESCAPES ME, LIKE THE BRAIN

Meaning still escapes me, like the brain
of a banana, like the gas that passes
out of the mouth of the month-old
cauliflower, like the jazz
that rises out of the tired bed
when I try too hard to sleep,
like the moon I carry in this wallet,
like the insistence on this very voice
of little interest to others, having given up
long ago on trying to please them—
that was a lip replacement that failed.

It still escapes me, this meaning in words,
like the dust of a comma, like a book
ruptured for eternity, like love
that reads itself to sleep,
like her hand that is a wave over me
when I stand alone in the night
and wander through this cedar house,
hoping that some golden conclusion
begins to burn in these eyes of winter,
that some final light landslides at last
into this simple longing.

Watching Episodes of *Unsolved Mysteries*

Watching episodes of *Unsolved Mysteries,*
I wait, anxiously, for the segment about me;
the one where family and friends, old lovers, colleagues,
looking confused and even sad, talk about
the day I simply disappeared.

Aging voices convince me that "He was the last person
in the world who would do this," that "Something terrible
has happened to him," and that his wallet,
left on the seat of his old Toyota, is sure evidence
that some evil has pressed upon him.

This heart begins to pound while I watch
the simulated videos, while I wait for the final
close-up pictures, the ones where I look just like
I always look, and the phone number at the bottom
of the screen, pleading for me to call.

The God We Pray to When We Think We Pray

The God we pray to when we think we pray
is not the God of Sleep,
not even God of Desperate Day.

These nights when sleep breaks me awake
to still another world of sleep,
I sit up in the dark, stuck once again
inside this middle ground of life, wondering
whose hand it was, like half a prayer,
that floated through the bed,
or what was in the box that was not there
before it fell and woke the worried dog.

All tests for sleep and wake
have always failed me—the pinch of skin,
the fingers racing for the light,
the bright reminders of a day-to-day
that does not shift and dance.

I look for words, like stars that might turn on;
I pray for something hard, to take me
back to more substantial space
where clocks are clocks, where time
hangs thick upon the walls.

All this longing life it seems the moon
alone has rescued me, its light
in scrambled darkness always singing,
"Clara Luna... Clara Luna... Clara Luna,"
loveliest of female tunes, turning me
to a dark and pagan peace
in this almost waking tale that is my life.

LIKE THE TONGUE OF A LONG LIZARD

Like the tongue of a long lizard, love
rolls out into the desert;
the sand, the trillion eyes of the universe,
undulates under the feet, gathers its force,
takes flight shortly after dusk;
and for a moment the mind recognizes
that it is recognized, and it, also,
rocks back and forth, back and
forth, finally breaking loose,
itself ocean and sand, night,
this mind, this constellation, this dew
falling on the deserted beach,
this cosmic sweat, these tear ducts
in the brain that sigh, that sing
dark stones, until the earth under these feet
is the very brain itself, the body
walking on its own sweet head,
like the strange feeling of inversion that
happens when we are very tired,
the strange weariness that happens
when we realize every grain of sand
is a letter in the alphabet we do not know
and can only know when we live in no
time, when we live in the sea that then is
only one drop in the cosmic ocean,
the water that is one cell
in the amoeba galaxy.

There, fish in old camps come out to see
the moon, come out to see the light that is
inside the light that strikes the simple eye;
and there, the memories of lilacs fifty years old
wash in, there the dream of being born
is like any other dream; and the old heart,
torn loose, begins its flap, like wild geese
with weather in their hearts, heading for
who knows what dream of south,
of no winter; there, like a watch
broken on the shore, the body stops,
and there is no age in the breath,
no age now in the universe, like the old woman
I saw in Alabama, hugging her banjo
when the playing stopped, like the wrinkles
on the baby the moment of birth; like
lightning that stops in its own motion and becomes
the time and space we know; like the desire
to tattoo our bodies with stars, or turn our limbs
into cottonwoods; or to find one simple word
and repeat it forever, not caring at all
what the word is, or what galaxy it is part of.

I Have Worked Hard to Make
the World Feel Solid

I have worked hard to make the world feel solid,
to say, "Yes, there is something under my feet,"
but still I feel a hole there when I step,
when one long leg sinks down toward the sun
at the center of the earth. Those weeks after I was born
I used every ounce of energy I could command
to come back to the body, to be here, and now,
and not in the world of rosy light.
It must have been a hard birth.

I was three years old before I convinced this mouth
to speak, to send out roots, to crawl with language
toward those strange faces suspended over me
like moons out of a mystery I had forgotten,
never understanding, to this very hour, what
conundrum I had been dropped into. Even now,
when someone waves, I see a hand inside the hand
waving, and another eye inside the eye, not knowing
which hand to wave to, or which eye to look into.

Why did I never worry that people did not
understand me, why did I tolerate their torture,
the mean blood of so many evil people,
why did this heart continue to kiss in secret
those who insisted that I suffer?
And why did this heart continue to kiss me in secret,
late at night, surviving like a voice in pure water,
this heart that loves pictures, and faces, and poems,
and jars of honey lined along the window?

In This Solitude Which is Never Really Solitude

In this solitude which is never really solitude,
in this familiar ritual of evening, I dance
around this body of mine, around this flesh still
unfamiliar to me, this mouth still being born,
this pair of faithful legs, these eyes that feel
phosphorescent when I sleep.

Things that make no sense to others
gather in these hands like baskets
filled with fish and multiplying roses,
like bread that has escaped destruction
because it was of little use to anyone but me,
like the thumb made for this right hand.

I remember when I stood quietly
at a cocktail party, staring at the hand
of the woman in front of me, fascinated
by those fingers that had been pulled into time.
She was angry she said because she thought
I did not want to look at her.

These are things impossible to explain.
Like trying to explain my dead grandmother's shoes
appearing before me one evening,
and then her ankles
wrapped in her sagging stockings,
wanting me to tie her shoes one more time.

It is like trying to explain what it is
to love someone, not because of cosmetics
but because of the wandering cosmos
in her words; like trying to explain
how light lives in the body
because the body was once a star.

It may be, after all, that I was born
and remain a lugubrious dyslexic,
unable to fathom into useful speech
the final thing—the here and now
and nothing but—but still there is the dance
the nothing here now blesses.

THIS STORY IS ABOUT FIRE AND DESTRUCTION

…no quiero hablar sino como es mi lengua.
Sal a buscar doctores si no te gusta el viento.

…I do not want to speak except as is my speech.
Go out and look for doctors if you don't like the wind.

—Pablo Neruda, "El Vino"

This story is about fire and destruction,
about the failure of all those who tried to strangle me
in their entrails, whose hearts were ashes,
whose bodies were lies, whose words were
labyrinths of seductive and decaying light, who,
like smugglers in the jungle stuffing cocaine
into the corpses of little children,
thought tenderness was something to be devoured.
Appropriate choices for fire and destruction.

But it was something in me destroyed,
and through that fire something not destroyed;
it was spirit surviving, living for years on rat shit,
lost on a sea with no shore, where bloated souls
rose up with wooden eyes, like mockeries of wives,
waving to me, reaching toward me with their sunken hands,
plucking pieces of this body, eating these legs I loved
when I was born, eating these very hands
that wove the light together my initial days on earth.

At last only one part of one ear remained,
but in that part the soul now concentrate
contained the genesis of the whole;
the evil that had fed on me had left
to find its fill in other, more fattening, waters.
I slept a very long time. When I woke
I heard some voices, as if a thousand years away
but human nevertheless, voices sounding
shore and hope immutable.

On that strange sand I flopped about
like a goblet of mangled flesh,
listening to words, to air hammered home;
words like banquets of food out of fairy tales,
words like milk to feed a warrior,
words that filled this solitary ear
like pollen out of heaven, words that walked
on earth with breath imperishable
and deaf to those who sought destruction.

With spring the ear grew fat and then the head grew back,
like a blessing that has made a long journey;
the heart, the heart began again
to move, to thump without a form, and then took root
in empty air and blossomed into body;
these feet, that looked at first so far away,
began to walk; and drop by sacred drop
the blood returned, and all the efforts of the damned
turned into simple dew that vanished with the sun.

I think I'll name a few of those who helped me through
the furious water; I'll name the bell that rang each breath
when once again I learned to speak and clumsily spell:
"Is a bel," a bell heard on the sea, and Doug and Nick
and James and Robert, saints to me,
and holy sisters Mabel, Nancy, Marilyn, Gerri,
all children in this fairy tale I live, where magic rises up
and catches me before I have been torn
too much to bring the body back.
Despite the dark the dawn is always being born.

ALL GOD'S EVENINGS GOT WINGS

All God's evenings got wings. Like the wing
on the back of the butterscotch cat
when he is sleeping, like the wing
on the long finger of Adam, or the shadow wing,
the wing of the past, or the green wing of the leaf,
or the long hair of the dead gathered into wing,
or the wedding wing when I think
of a woman I love, or the wing of a poem
when it rises out of defeat, or the singing wing
of the little child, running lopsided
through streets of no wing, or the wing of the sticks
in the I-Ching, or the wing over the shacks
hidden in the skirts of Lima, or the wing
of happiness when we realize that all flesh
is lovely, or the wing that watches over me
when it is two-thirty in the morning and I would
give any wing to be with you.

Through Some Ill-Fitting Time and Space

Through some ill-fitting time and space
he wandered, carrying in a pack
what tenderness and little bread he had
until the bread was gone, at last arriving
only to this: a love that had no skin,
no rocking bed, no breakfast by the sea.

But what if he on earth was born
to find the woman of his heart
and love her greatly? What matter
then that space disjointed conjured all
against him? What matter then
the loneliness of flesh?

What if the one fine purpose
of his poor and complicated life
had been to wander through
the masquerades of love, the mean
and lowly lies, deceits, and empty hearts,
and still survive?

Yes, survive, despite the brutal wives,
their lives of lies and callous laughter,
survive to seek what he had always sought,
so much that no career and nothing
of importance ever happened in his life,
but this:

He found the woman of his heart
and loved her greatly; loved her so
that in a thousand years some dusty scholar
might unearth some letters, gentle lines
of love as in the ancient lore, and pausing
for a moment to think,

This was a man who found the woman
of his heart, and loved her greatly.

WHEN ALL THE THERAPISTS OF DUNG ARE GATHERED

When all the therapists of dung are gathered
on the dying hill for one last dance,
when all the schools of brain are dead,
when all the seas, exhausted, turn to dust,
I still will sing to you, because you are
the wheat that rose up into bread
when most I needed it; because you are
the cinnamon on celestial tongues,
the auburn sky above this peasant blood—
this blood of Quaker blacksmiths,
this blood of mediums still wandering—
because you are the delicate flower
I found in the crack of ferocious day.

Out of the simple longings of this old soul
I sing these clumsy songs to you,
like bells giving birth through the white hair
of night, because you are, because
this thump of heart thinks more of you
than of the Goddess and her own sweet rump,
because this is human love, and not simply
a story of being in love; I will sing to you
because, for me, you are, until
these words themselves turn into tiny birds
that weave amid the moving tapestries of sleep;
and when these strong brown hands have turned
again to earth, they still will blossom with your name.

ON THIS HIGH MESA I KEEP A LOW PROFILE

On this high mesa I keep a low profile,
living alone, like a language broken loose,
with this address: "General Delivery,
Glade Park, Colorado," obstinately sticking
to some decoction of sound and desert sage,
while age begins to creep up around me,
like hushed sighs heard in the middle of the night.

I know that I do not have enough dolphins
and shamans in these poems, only
the dull fins of night fish floundering
in a simple sky, in this red sea
of the sad heart; I know well
this intense passion for doing nothing,
for having no popular focus.

Decades ago I thought there was a piece
missing in the soft gray stone, in the mush
of matter that this soul, in time, ticked through;
and I thought I might find that
mystery, the way one might find a mate
standing at the gate of some wooden castle
along the road of interminable longing.

Who knows what God and his idiot brother
may yet bring to me, but bring it now ·
I say, I pray, I lay me down to weep;
give me something now however faint.
This life is like trying to win a three-legged race
when your partner is a kindly
but slow moving saint.

About the Author

James Tipton lives with his wife Martha and his daughter Gabriela in the tropical mountains of central Mexico in the town of Chapala, south of Guadalajara. His collection of poems, *Letters from a Stranger* (Conundrum Press, 1999), with a foreword by Isabel Allende, won the Colorado Book Award. He has a particular interest in short poems and short (including flash) fiction. A collection of haiku, *Proposing to the Woman in the Rear View Mirror,* was published in October 2008, and a collection of tanka, five-line poems, *All the Horses of Heaven* was published in January 2009 by Modern English Tanka Press.